T0146877

# SEVENTEEN SYLLABLES

## A Poetic Glimpse of Life

Haiku and Graphics

Diantha Ain

**SEVENTEEN SYLLABLES**
**A POETIC GLIMPSE OF LIFE**



*iUniverse books may be ordered through booksellers or by contacting:*

*iUniverse*
*1663 Liberty Drive*
*Bloomington, IN 47403*
*www.iuniverse.com*
*1-800-Authors (1-800-288-4677)*



*ISBN: 978-1-5320-0327-1 (sc)*
*ISBN: 978-1-5320-0328-8 (e)*

*Library of Congress Control Number: 2016911924*

*Print information available on the last page.*

*iUniverse rev. date: 08/01/2016*

For my husband Bob,
whose love and devotion have
inspired me for more than sixty-five years,

# Preface

Haiku is a traditional Japanese poetry form. It is usually written in the present or future tense with no more than seventeen syllables: five in the first line, seven in the second, and five in the third. Haiku captures a special moment.

The red pictograph on the cover is a traditional signature stamp of my name in international Japanese. The wooden stamp is called a *han*.

When I first started writing haiku in 1980, it was a very personal discovery for me, and I rarely shared them. When I was asked to expound on them at meeting of The National League of American Women, to which I belonged, Virginia Anderson, a retired master teacher and poet, highly praised my work. It was her words of encouragement that led me to writing a collection of one hundred haiku, which I printed myself on fourfold greeting cards and stamped with the signature *han* that I had ordered from Japan. She included my haiku in two of the four poetry books she published under the title *DAYbreak*

My friend, Margaret Brownley, a romance novelist, lost her eldest son at age 31. The grief affected her family members so severely, she set out to write a comforting grief book. She sent surveys to people who could offer insight into how losses had affected their lives. As I was completing my survey, it stirred strong emotions in me that inspired haiku. Upon reading them, Margaret asked me to collaborate with her on the book, *Grieving God's Way.* As a promotional scheme, she contacted *Bereavement: A Magazine of Hope and Healing,* which published individual sections of the book, and I became their haiku editor for five years. I sent them hundreds of haiku, and they carefully selected several each month to complement articles to be published.

Martha Bolton, another friend and talented writer, asked me to write haiku for a grief book she was writing for young people, *Saying Goodbye When You Don't Want To.* Her book covered a variety of losses, not just deaths. Losing a friendship or a pet, moving to a new town, or dealing with divorce, all inflict emotions similar to grief.

Jennifer Rairigh, Director of Camp Courage, a grief camp for kids and teens in NE Pennsylvania, chose a haiku from Martha's book that she wanted permission to put on T-shirts for the campers. I, of course, was delighted to give her my blessings, and she sent me one of the shirts as a thank-you.

Gail Small, a retired teacher, motivational speaker, scholar, and friend, invited me to send a collection for her book, *Joyful Parenting,* and she made them one of the chapters in the book.

For several years, I went to a local elementary school to teach fourth, fifth, and sixth graders to write haiku. My friend, Mildred Karasik, was their teacher and displayed the good ones, of which there were many, on the school bulletin board.

My Japanese friend, Denzo Hosoi, who likes me to call him James, was touched by the six haiku that were included in my memoir, *My Roots and Blossoms: In Chapter and Verse.* He quoted two of them in his return letters to me. I accept that as a genuine Japanese "stamp of approval."

I extend my heartfelt thanks to everyone who has encouraged my writing haiku and enjoyed the results. Over the years, I have probably written more than a thousand haiku. I truly feel they are a gift to me, and I happily regift them to you readers.

# My Graphics

My graphics evolved from creating designs for original Christmas cards. In 1985, I wanted to use a haiku for my greeting, and I wanted it to be the first thing to be seen, so I created a fancy first letter to be printed in red to tie in with the red pictograph of my name, which would be at the end. It read:

Now it's the season
for our hearts to reunite
with love and greetings.

As they opened the card, my graphic design of two interwoven red hearts appeared, one spelling MERRY and the other spelling CHRISTMAS. The reactions I received from my friends were so gratifying that I decided to put graphic designs on the front of my cards, and I continued for nearly thirty years.

There was always a bit of mystery for my recipients, as I shaped a word into an impression of the message I wanted my card to convey. The word LOVE represented a Christmas tree for the first card, and now I've chosen it for the first category in this book. It is also a framed needlepoint in my dining room, done by a man who had put the first design on a pin cushion as a Christmas gift for me the year before. I have four others he did for me hung in my art room.

The year I turned the word love into a Madonna and child, I got the most fascinating reactions. Some people saw only the Madonna image, others saw only the word love, and the exceptional few saw both. These reactions only inspired me to create greater challenges for people. The message inside that card was: Christmas is a labor of love.

May you enjoy the challenge each haiku category presents to you. Some are more intricate than others, but I hope you can figure each one out as you come to it.

# Table of Contents

Mundane chores become
joyful experiences
when done for loved ones.

Love expands itself
to a greater dimension
when given away.

No birds nor flowers
need proclaim the joy of spring,
for I am in love.

Empty words of love
penetrate the human heart
and tear it to shreds.

Love is not contrived,
it happens, like conception,
when the time is right.

The power of love
lives on beyond the people
who have shared its joy.

When we fall in love,
our finest instincts emerge
for the world to see.

The magic of love
works mysteriously to
change lives forever.

Pleasant memories,
preserved in love, grow sweeter
each time they're savored.

Contented kittens
learn the joy of mother love
from a prickly tongue.

Two lives become one
in purpose and destiny
with one simple vow.

God's mantle of love
is always there to warm us
when the world grows cold.

Let home be a nest
feathered deep in love and trust
where wings can be stretched.

Love connects people
in an invisible way
that's quite amazing.

Love is bountiful,
offering the best rewards
to the most sincere.

The wonder of love
is its power to maintain
immortality.

The color of love
is visible only to
those who are smitten.

A dozen roses
can clearly say I love you
in any language.

Love's a precious gift
we give to those whom we choose,
with no guarantees.

Let a valentine
express the loving feelings
you can't verbalize.

Perfect moments are
when we share something we love
with someone we love.

Your loving whispers,
are like beautiful music,
nourishing my soul.

Love is a rocket
that blasts us from the mundane
to the euphoric.

Love is life's honey,
sweetening everyone
who comes in contact.

The art of romance
gives life a vibrant color
that glows in the dark.

Romance changes us,
much as a prism turns light
into a rainbow.

While romance sparks love,
tenderness and commitment
fan eternal flames.

As likenesses fuse
and differences resolve,
romance flourishes.

Romance elevates
human spirits to new heights
envied by the stars.

Romantic notions
are the otters that frolic
in the sea of love.

When two souls entwine
in a romantic setting,
Eden is reborn.

On the road to love,
the handsomest carriage is
a golden romance.

When two lives unite,
their pulsing hearts may create
wild syncopation.

Romantics live life
in joyous celebration
of their existence.

Real magic happens
when romance touches your heart
with its gentle wand.

Fantasies and dreams
pantomime reality
as romance unfolds.

Violin music
sends the feeling of romance
wafting through the air.

The euphoric sense
of all things being in place
makes romance ideal.

The spell romance casts
joins two people together
like Siamese twins.

Romance titillates,
rousing a sleepy giant
disguised as hormones.

The sexes attract,
drawn by uncontrollable
innate enticement.

Passion crescendos
as songs of romance echo
from your heart to mine.

Love is the beacon
that guides rudderless romance
to a safe harbor.

Romance just happens
at any given moment
without a warning.

Emotions erupt,
spewing passions on paper
in romance novels.

A single red rose
is the epitome of
a blooming romance.

The joy of romance
is its fantasies of love
that nurture the soul.

A perfect romance
merges two loving people
into one couple.

FRIENDS

Friendship is the boat
that stabilizes our ride
on life's roughest seas.

The love of a friend
turns life's unicycle to
a joyful tandem.

Friends are the rewards
God scatters throughout our lives,
to find and treasure.

Strong friendships are built
with continuous layers
of understanding.

Compassionate friends
know the art of listening
with their ears and hearts.

Friendship represents
the finest qualities of
our humanity.

Gardens and friendships
demand and reciprocate
tender loving care.

In times of trial
my friends are like a fortress,
giving me comfort.

Experiences
become precious memories
when shared with dear friends.

When we build a bridge
joining one to another,
both are made stronger.

Let me touch your life,
for then mine will be enriched
from that moment on.

Colorful people
blend their beauty to create
the rainbow of life.

Just a look or smile
can relay inner feelings
between longtime friends.

Friendship provides us
a comforting oasis
on our trek through life.

Our friends ripen life,
adding sweetness and texture
to our destiny.

Good relationships
bring out the best features of
individuals.

Friendship's a haven
where hearts can expose themselves
to the light of truth.

The tides of friendship
give us the support we need
when waters run deep.

Our hearts remain one
though time and space divide us,
because we are friends.

When I see balloons,
memories of happy times
always drift to you.

Our true friends accept
both our strengths and weaknesses
without any qualms.

Understanding friends
provide an invisible
life-support system.

Good relationships
can build a firm foundation
with our commitment.

Time is a treasure
that increases in value
when we're together.

Nature offers us
a perpetual wellspring
of inspiration.

Bright Iceland poppies
burst like silken butterflies
from pale green cocoons.

Shrewd chameleons
survive in a changing world
by changing with it.

Ominous gray clouds
prophesy stormy weather
chased by a rainbow.

Pale silvery trails
from here to a hideaway
measure a snail's pace.

The sun in the west
paints a masterpiece for me,
then steals it away.

Aspen trees shiver
with the first chill of winter,
then glow like sunshine.

Eucalyptus trees
discard crusty coats of bark
like molting reptiles.

Spores drift on the wind,
trusting they will land safely
upon fertile ground.

Wildflowers blossom,
assuring a doubtful world
desert life persists.

Moonlight softens night,
hiding mundane ugliness
while lighting the stars.

Only centipedes
need extend a hundred feet
to travel an inch.

Bold chrysanthemums
harbor in their pungency
eternal autumn.

Willows weep softly
into a receding lake
as summer departs.

Silently snow falls,
disguising Mother Nature
in a cloak of white.

Acorns lay dreaming
in the shadow of an oak
they will emulate.

In this frantic world
of ever increasing speed,
snails set their own pace.

Flaming zinnias
transform my verdant garden
to a bright palette.

As petals open,
Mother Nature's artistry
goes on exhibit.

Shadows merge with stripes
as tree and tiger become
one with the jungle.

Vivid fuchsia bursts,
saddled on clumps of green leaves,
ride the spring breezes.

Butterflies worship
in a portable chapel
borne by stained glass wings.

A thin crescent moon
cuts through the ebony sky
to give me a smile.

Mushrooms demonstrate
what growth possibilities
lie in dark places.

Life

Life is a concert
we must conduct with our own
rhythm and tempo.

If the choice is yours,
gather the courage to take
the road less traveled.

To accomplish deeds,
we must begin with our dreams,
giving each one life.

Each new beginning
is an opportunity
to excel in life.

Birthdays are milestones
that merely mark our progress
on the road of life.

Raindrops and teardrops
wash away the grittiness
of daily living.

High on a hillside,
where the earth and sky unite,
I find contentment.

Believe in yourself,
to show other people how
to believe in you.

Moments of anger
fill the world with flint-like sparks
that sear our psyches.

Along life's highway,
a fresh horizon appears
with each forward stride.

The finger of time
moves on continually,
waiting for no one.

Beautiful moments
flit in and out of each life
like a butterfly.

Beneath book covers,
lie wonderful unknown worlds
waiting to be found.

The pains of past years
prepare our emotions for
future dilemmas.

As autumn leaves fall,
we brace for the winter storm
while dreaming of spring.

Tenderness is learned
by watching loving people
demonstrate the art.

Chinese expertise
creates magical moments
through well-placed needles.

The hazards of life
must not deter our efforts
to reach for the stars.

Family ties bind
the willing and unwilling
in life's tug-of-war.

The joy of good health
is best appreciated
when we are not well.

Life's curriculum
always includes tough courses
we'd rather not take.

Human bitterness
slowly erodes the vessel
that preserves its bile.

Cherish this moment,
for it will be quickly gone,
never to return.

Let each day unfold
like the petals of a rose,
high above the thorns.

Creativity
allows our finest instincts
to take dimension.

Creating one's own
indomitable spirit
may take a lifetime.

Creative children
have direct taproots to their
imaginations.

Simple solutions
are most often discovered
accidentally.

Creative muscles
demand regular workouts
for self-maintenance.

Creativity
materializes our
imagination.

On life's carousel,
those who stretch their potential
acquire the brass ring.

Creativity
flows like the sap in a tree,
giving paper life.

Creative living
allows mundane chores to have
an artistic flair.

Fantasies allow
impossibilities to
become plausible.

Creative moments
may awaken us from sleep
at alarming times.

Windows of the mind
offer panoramic views
to visionaries.

Beautiful music
puts the soul in the mood for
creativity.

My creative sparks
flicker, ignite, then explode,
lighting up my life.

Creativity
will blossom like a flower,
if cultivated.

Outrageous moments
allow free spirits leeway
to be creative.

Quilting turns fabric
into artistic heirlooms
that warm people's hearts.

Creative thinking
offers us alternative
means of survival

The art of living
is perfected by probing
the new and unknown.

Creativity
flows from one to another
unpredictably.

The precise science
of meteorology
tries to outguess God.

Creativity
offers each of us a chance
to be outstanding.

My mind's a fishbowl,
where creative ideas
swim and develop.

Creativity
is the delicious frosting
on life's birthday cake.

Poetry frames words,
creating, on occasion,
a real masterpiece.

Ideas transfer
from one soul to another
meter by meter.

As poets weave words,
the fabric they create gains
color and texture.

Vintage poetry
aged in emotional kegs,
intoxicates me.

Weighty verbiage
balances thoughts and feelings …
poetic justice.

Poetry gains life
as emotions circulate
from pen to paper.

Poets capture words
in deftly gilded cages
where their song resounds.

Poetry provides
an outstanding platform for
imagination.

Verbal gymnastics
stretch the possibilities
for a poet's mind.

Poetry whispers
powerful words of wisdom
that make my soul shriek.

Poets elevate
the seamy side of life with
beautiful language.

Thought provoking words,
moving along in meter,
create poetry.

Poets sculpt each word,
masterfully creating
life-shaped passages.

Poets paint the page
with bold verbal expressions
that spark mental fires.

Poets bare their souls
with the blatant disregard
of nude centerfolds.

Writing poetry
offers us do-it-yourself
trauma therapy.

Poetic talent
must be unwrapped carefully
and honed forever.

Odes paint an image
of a person or object
deserving of praise.

Poetry transforms
commonplace words and phrases
to musical sounds.

Children will absorb
the rhythm and fun of words
taught with poetry.

Reading poetry
offers a respite from pain
through words of wisdom.

Words gain new power
once they are relegated
to poetic form.

Poetry creates
a pulsating ebb and flow
of connected thoughts.

Haiku offers us
a simple means to acquire
mental clarity.

ART

The art of living
can only be mastered by
trial and error.

Measure by measure,
composers build melodies
with uncounted notes.

As an artist paints,
each careful movement becomes
a stroke of genius.

Interpretive dance
relates a beautiful tale
in body language.

Musical drama
sends the audience away
humming the plot lines.

An art gallery
allows artists' works to be
seen in their best light.

In a sculptor's hands,
shapeless lumps of clay acquire
an eternal life.

Muralists create
colorful new scenic worlds
stretching wall to wall.

Mimes mesmerize us
with fluid body movements
that speak silently.

Orchestras combine
the artistry of many
to create one sound.

When fingers touch keys,
the soul of a pianist
turns to melody.

Topiary art
shapes Mother Nature to suit
snippy gardeners.

Artists recreate
what man and God have designed
with new dimension.

Totem poles depict
history and family
blended into art.

Characters in books
gain life through the hard labor
of gifted writers.

Chain saw sculptors buzz
through giant logs to create
artwork and sawdust.

Rhetorical skill
gives simple words the power
of persuasiveness.

Auto designers
integrate the driving wind
into molded steel.

We all need to learn
the art of relaxation
to survive this world.

Creative writing
breathes believability
into fantasy.

A *chef de cuisine*
turns common green groceries
to masterpieces.

One artists' model
becomes multiple people
before the class ends.

Persevering toes
elevate ballerinas
to heights of stardom.

Family portraits
perpetuate the living
and preserve the dead.

HUMOR

Laughter keeps us sane
in a world that endeavors
to drive us crazy.

Neon and good taste
are not ordinarily
found on the same sign.

People who love sports
seem to spend most of their time
watching others play.

More stitches are found
lifting folks' faces these days
than darning their socks.

My ideal diet
would drop more bulk from my hips
than from my wallet.

Men and women talk,
using similar words with
different meanings.

On a grocer's shelf,
the Spanish olives marked large
are the smallest size.

Patients see doctors,
but in order to do so,
they must have patience.

Robots work out well,
'cause they don't need potty breaks
and don't drink coffee.

The joy of laughter
can be more contagious than
the Asian flu bug.

"Easy Assembly"
leads many a sane person
to pulling out hair.

To pay my taxes,
I keep myself constantly
overtaxed at work.

Fashion designers
strive each year to captivate
our dollars and sense.

At a restaurant,
I wonder impatiently,
who's waiting on whom?

My smoke detector
serves mostly as a critic
of my bad cooking.

While we're striving for
political correctness,
common sense flounders.

When all attempts fail,
leaving me at my wits' end,
I read directions.

Professional jocks
demonstrate an urge to kill
in a sporting way.

"Till death do us part"
gives us ample time to learn
to live together.

Respect for elders
is required of young children,
but not workplaces.

The news of the day
loses much power and depth
through lightweight anchors.

Some think it's funny
when we commit a major
*faux pas* in public.

Beavers destroy trees
to build lodges in rivers
that make dam good homes.

The gift of humor
comes from serious writers
who don't clown around.

THANKS

When saying thank you,
a tiny part of oneself
is given away.

Warm thanks build a bridge
to a generous spirit
from a grateful heart.

Joy and gratitude
make my cup runneth over
spilling thanks to you.

No song is so sweet,
no lyric quite so joyful
as a hymn of thanks.

Like a bird soaring
with simple grace and beauty,
my thanks fly to you.

Thanks form a vessel
filled with love and gratitude
that pours out freely.

Thanks generate warmth
in the heart of the donor
and recipient.

My heartstrings respond
to your generous spirit
by echoing thanks.

Thank you embodies
the noblest qualities of
the human spirit.

Words of gratitude
complete a circle of joy
begun by a gift.

My thanks waft to you
on the gentle flowing tones
of my piano.

A simple thank you
from a loving, grateful heart
is a gift itself.

When good things happen
that are unexplainable,
I know whom to thank.

Generosity
plants the seeds of gratitude
which grow vines of love.

Words of thanks create
an atmosphere of sunshine
that brightens the day.

Your extreme kindness
should be rewarded by my
superfluous thanks.

Thank you seasons life
with a delicate flavor
that sweetens the soul.

A smile or gesture
can compound the power of
a simple thank you.

My thanks bubble up
with champagne effervescence
in a toast to you.

The joy of a gift
magnifies and beautifies
when thanks are exchanged.

A verbal bouquet
may be wrapped in simple words ...
thank you very much.

Warm thanks pierce the heart
leaving warm embers behind
that last a lifetime.

My thanks dance your way
in a graceful pirouette
that reflects my joy.

The color of thanks
is vibrant and beautiful
as a spring morning.

FAITH

My faith is a kite
that carries me to the heights,
where I talk to God.

Of all our blessings,
the ability to love
is God's greatest gift.

Hope springs eternal,
but we must fill up our cups
to drink deep of it.

Thunder and lightning
boldly remind each of us
where the power lies.

My faith is defined
by the actions I pursue
as I live each day.

The light of the moon
reminds me how constantly
God's love lights my life.

Faith provides a shield
to protect me as I face
the battles of life.

When I think I'm lost,
I stop briefly to check for
angels unaware.

When we form a chain,
our prayers have the power to
create miracles.

Faith is the cushion
that protects our fragile souls
on life's bumpy road.

We must put more faith
in our own abilities
than in lotteries.

Worldly temptations
exercise my growing faith,
keeping it supple.

Let God touch your life,
for then you will be enriched
from that moment on.

God's mantle of love
is always there to warm us
when the world grows cold.

With faith, comes power
to live life to the fullest,
making dreams come true.

Our losses in life
teach us to appreciate
the gifts that God gives.

God's dearest angels
serve His divine purposes
among the living.

As I kneel to pray,
the measured moments of time
become infinite.

Saying nightly prayers
gives me a chance to recount
my daily blessings.

God's love is a gift
designed to fortify us
from tribulation.

God lights up my day
more brightly than the sunshine
blazing in the sky.

The good in our hearts
is not of our own making,
but where God abides.

Seasons come and go,
but God's love is like the sun
constantly shining.

Forgiving someone
is a precious gift to them
as well as ourselves.

Grief is impartial,
equally allotting pain
to beggars and kings.

Photograph albums
offer us a chance to see
lost loves smile again.

Waves of emotion
sink and swell with sudden force,
testing survivors.

Tears comfort the soul,
washing away our sorrow
one drop at a time.

Life's painful moments
nourish the inner fiber
that forms our backbones.

Death drops a curtain
on one act of life's drama,
but the play goes on.

Love is bittersweet
when those who share its delights
are parted by fate.

When lungs are stricken
with overpowering grief,
each breath drowns in tears.

My spirit wanders
on a nomadic search for
an answer to death.

Love letters to you
are carefully encoded
within my journal.

I talk to myself
about things other people
are afraid to say.

Living in the past
is an impossible feat
that limits today.

Great loss in our life
makes us appreciate more
life's simple pleasures.

For recovery,
we personally design
our rite of passage.

From the beginning,
we are dependent upon
other people's love.

We search for rainbows,
but we must weather a storm
before we see one.

Only hand in hand
can we guide one another
through life's dilemmas.

Grief paralyzes
the emotional muscles
that shape our judgment.

The meaning of life
can be understood only
by accepting death.

My sorrow plays out
as a piano etude
in a minor key.

The laying of hands
miraculously eases
the pain of grieving.

Life's simple pleasures
remind me to continue
as if you were here.

Death is the climax
to the symphony we write
as our life plays out.

Let us celebrate
the wonderful gift of life
in our toast to death.

# Acknowledgments

The man who did six of my graphic designs in needlepoint is Phillip Crouch. They have become treasures for me, and I couldn't possibly thank him enough.

The talented women who helped me finish this book in the best possible way are Cheryl Talbot, Margaret Brownley, and Alexis O'Neill.

Cheryl Talbot is a former English teacher, poet, actress, composer and lyricist. Margaret Brownley is a New York Times Best Selling Author of forty books of fiction. Alexis O'Neill is the published author of five children's books and has spent innumerable hours visiting children in schools, encouraging their creativity and interest in reading.

All three of these women have been there for me when I needed them. My thanks seem insufficient considering what they have given me over the years, but they are heartfelt and sincere.

Printed in the United States
By Bookmasters